FLORENCE
NIGHTINGALE

What Made Them Great

FLORENCE
NIGHTINGALE

What Made Them Great

Donna Shore

Illustrated by Gianni Renna

SILVER BURDETT PRESS

ACKNOWLEDGMENTS

We would like to thank Martha Vicinus, Professor Emeritus, Department of English, University of Michigan; and Jacqueline Gorton, Librarian, Gill/St. Bernards School for their guidance and helpful suggestions.

Project Editor: Emily Easton (Silver Burdett Press)

Adapted and reformatted from the original by Kirchoff/Wohlberg, Inc.

Project Director: John R. Whitman
Graphics Coordinator: Jessica A. Kirchoff
Production Coordinator: Marianne Hile

Library of Congress Cataloging-in-Publication Data

Shore, Donna, 1934—
    Florence Nightingale/Donna Shore; illustrated by Gianni Renna.
    p. cm.—[FROM SERIES: What Made Them Great]

Adaptation of: Florence Nightingale/Donnali Shor; translated by Donna Shore.
    © 1987 Silver Burdett Company, Morristown, New Jersey.
    [FROM SERIES: Why They Became Famous]
    Includes bibliographical references.
Summary: Recounts the life story of the English girl who became a famous nurse and dedicated
    herself to the alleviation of suffering at home and abroad.
    1. Nightingale, Florence, 1820-1910—Juvenile literature. 2. Nurses— England—Biography—
    Juvenile literature. [1. Nightingale, Florence, 1820-1910. 2. Nurses.] I. Renna, Gianni, ill.
    II. Title. III. Series.

RT37.N5S48 1990   610.73'092—dc20   [B]   [92]   89-38647   CIP   AC

© Gruppo Editoriale Fabbri S.p.A. 1987
Translated into English by Donna Shore for Silver Burdett Press
First published in the United States by Silver Burdett Press under license of Gruppo Editoriale Fabbri S.p.A.

10 9 8 7 6 5 4 3 2 1 (Library Binding)
10 9 8 7 6 5 4 3 2 1 (Softcover)

ISBN 0-382-09978-8 (Library Binding)
ISBN 0-382-24004-9 (Softcover)

TABLE OF CONTENTS

Florence's Childhood

ne of the most charming cities in the world is Florence, in Italy. There, Florence Nightingale was born on May 12, 1820. Fanny Nightingale, the mother of the new baby, loved the city.

Of all European cities, Florence was perhaps the liveliest. Every night there were parties and fancy balls. She adored attending the opera. The beautiful Fanny was invited everywhere.

William Edward Nightingale, the baby's father, also enjoyed the city. But his reasons were different. He was a quiet man who spent his time reading and studying. There was much to learn in Florence. It was his favorite place, too. So, when

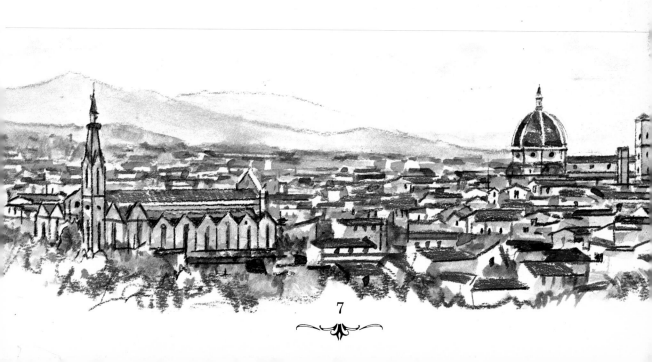

Fanny wanted to go there for the birth of their child, he was delighted.

The Nightingales were a rich English couple. Like other people of wealth, they took great pleasure in traveling. After their marriage, they went to Europe. For several years, they toured the continent. In southern Italy, they first lived in the city of Naples. There, Fanny had given birth to a daughter.

Fanny must have been a romantic woman. She liked unusual names. Her first child was named Parthenope. This was the Greek word for Naples. She also decided to call her second daughter after the city of her birth. In 1820, few girls were named Florence. But within Florence Nightingale's lifetime, it became popular all over the world. Of course, this was because thousands of baby girls were named in honor of her.

The Nightingales returned to England when Florence was one year old. Her sister Parthe was two.

Life in the Nightingale household was pleasant. There were pets of all sorts—ponies, birds, cats, and dogs. And there were even different homes for the different seasons. During the summers, the family lived at Lea Hurst. This large country house had fifteen bedrooms. It was designed by Florence's father.

They also owned a winter home, called Embley. Mrs. Nightingale preferred living at Embley. It was near her friends and relatives. Having company was

fun. She invited lots of guests, who often stayed for weeks at a time. Fanny also liked the parties given by people in high society. Twice a year, the family made trips to London. Fanny attended all the balls.

Life was confortable and carefree. Florence and Parthenope were lucky little girls. They had everything money could buy. By nature, the two sisters—who called each other Flo and Parthe—were very different. Parthe took after her mother. She loved good times. In the large gardens at Lea Hurst she liked to ride her pony.

But Florence was happiest sitting quietly and reading. Like her father, she tended to be shy and serious. She was bright and pretty and she moved gracefully. Her eyes were large and gray. Her shiny brown hair was the color of chestnuts. But she had a stubborn streak. Sometimes it made people feel a little uneasy. Of the two sisters, Parthe was the one people usually liked better.

There were few people whom Florence really trusted. When she liked someone, she gave one hundred percent of her affection. In return, she expected the same. Her favorite person happened to be Aunt Mai, her father's sister.

One day Florence would never forget was her seventh birthday. Her family was visiting London. On this lovely spring day, the sun shone brightly. After unwrapping gifts, the Nightingales went out for a walk. At Kensington Palace, Florence's father stopped. He pointed to the royal home.

"Princess Victoria lives there," he told Florence. "She's only a year older than you. Her birthday is in May, too."

How proud Florence felt. She shared her birthday month with a princess. Some day, Victoria might even become queen of England.

"They call the princess little May flower," Mr. Nightingale said. "But you are my May flower."

On this perfect day, Florence was feeling so happy. She skipped along gaily between her parents. Suddenly, her mother said, "I've got a special surprise for you. Aunt Mai is to be married. And you're going to be one of her bridesmaids."

To Mrs. Nightingale's surprise, Florence burst into tears. "No, I won't let her!" she sobbed. "She can't leave us." Her parents tried to calm her. They promised that Aunt Mai would love both her husband and Florence. But Florence refused to be comforted. News of her aunt's plans completely spoiled her birthday.

The summer passed. Gradually, Florence began to accept the idea of her aunt's marriage. On the day of the wedding, the bride glowed with happiness. This made Florence feel even worse. She was losing the only person who truly understood her. Who would be as nice to her as Aunt Mai?

At the church, the bride and groom knelt before the altar. Suddenly, Florence tearfully rose to her feet. Before anyone could stop her, she ran up and knelt between the couple. But Aunt Mai didn't mind. She knew that her niece wanted to be close. So she reached over and put her arm around Florence. Later, Florence looked back on this day. It was both the happiest day of her life—and the saddest.

In those years, Florence began to jot down her feelings in a diary. Or, she scribbled secret thoughts on little bits of paper. If she wanted to remember something important, she reached for a scrap of paper, or an envelope, or anything at hand. All her life, she continued this habit. These "private notes," as she would describe them, were never thown away either.

In her writings, she could talk about her deepest feelings. There were some things she dared not tell anyone, not even Aunt Mai. Florence believed she was different from other little girls. She had a secret fear, and it terrified her. She worried that she might be a monster.

Each morning, she rushed to her mirror. Had her face changed during the night? Were there bumps to give her away? Meeting new people scared her. Perhaps, they might discover her awful secret.

One day, some of her cousins arrived for tea. Mrs. Nightingale and Parthe hurried downstairs to meet them. Parthe was wearing her nicest gown. Her mother promised she could help with the special tea cups they always used for company. Mr. Nightingale came into the parlor for a few minutes. But after saying hello, he went back to the library.

"Where's Flo?" asked Mrs. Nightingale. "Her tea is getting cold. Soon there won't be any cakes left."

Parthe knew her mother was annoyed. Florence was ruining the party. Parthe raced upstairs. She found Florence sitting at her desk.

"Hurry up," Parthe called out. "Everyone is waiting for you. Mother's getting angry."

Florence shook her head. "Don't want to," she said. Her expression was stubborn.

"You must come down. Our cousins brought their friends to meet us."

"I won't like them," Florence insisted. "And I bet they won't like me."

Parthe never liked her sister's moods. Usually, they happened when company came. Only an hour ago, Florence had been smiling as she did multiplication tables. That sounded boring to Parthe. Weren't tea and cakes much more fun? Parthe did not understand Flo. But she knew one thing. If her sister didn't come down soon, they would both get into trouble.

Finally, Parthe began to plead. "I'll give you a piece of my cake," she promised.

But Florence sat frozen in her chair. She felt miserable. She realized that her mother was losing patience. Why couldn't she be nice like Parthe? But when guests came, she wanted to run away and hide. Still, Florence knew she had better join the others.

Tea parties bored Florence. So did putting on company manners. It was far more interesting to study mathematics. And it was more useful. Ever since her governess had explained what could be done with numbers, Florence was eager to learn more.

Now, her favorite word was "useful." If she liked something, she would call it useful. Unlike tea parties, useful things had a purpose. Florence was happiest when she had something interesting to do. Then, she would work very hard.

But sometimes there was absolutely nothing to do. Then, she felt miserable.

Learning was one of her greatest pleasures. When Florence was twelve, Mr. Nightingale decided to teach the girls himself. In those days, it was unusual to send girls to school. Rich families expected their daughters to play the piano and paint pretty pictures. Intellectual activities were believed to be unsuitable for young ladies.

But Mr. Nightingale was a different sort of father. He thought it was important for girls to have good educations. So, he began to give Parthe and Florence lessons in history and philosophy. He taught them five languages, including Greek and Latin.

In this matter of the girls' schooling, Fanny Nightingale did not agree with her husband. There were frequent quarrels about it. She often said that learning so many subjects was not necessary at all. Why did a young lady have to read Latin? To be accomplished, all she needed was a knowledge of music and art. But the lessons went on just the same.

One summer afternoon, Florence and Parthe were sitting in class. Outside, birds sang. It was a lovely sunny day. Mr. Nightingale was reading a story from an Italian book.

Parthe had trouble paying attention. She found the story dull. Her mind wandered. Only one more hour to go, she thought. Then, she could help arrange flowers with her mother. That evening, there was to be a dinner party. Parthe could not help yawning.

Suddenly, her father laid down the book. He turned to Parthe. "What do you think of the story?"

Parthe's cheeks turned pink. "Could you repeat the last part?" she stammered. "I...I couldn't hear very well."

"You couldn't hear me because you weren't listening."

Parthe hung her head.

"All week, you haven't paid attention," Mr. Nightingale said. His voice rose. "Since you're not going to study, you may as well leave!"

Parthe felt ashamed. Putting away her books, she ran from the room. She knew her father was upset. But luckily her mother would not care. Mrs. Nightingale never scolded when lessons were neglected. Sometimes she even encouraged it. If the Nightingales were having a party, Mrs. Nightingale would insist that she needed Parthe's help. On those occasions, she managed to get her daughter excused from classes.

After Parthe had left, Mr. Nightingale shrugged his shoulders. He sighed and turned to Florence. "Let's begin our history lesson," he said. "Open your book to the chapter on Egypt."

This chapter described the pyramids. Excited, Florence reached for the book. History was one of her favorite subjects. People who lived long ago always fascinated her. Reading about their lives was more thrilling than reading a made-up story. She wanted to find out all about their houses and the objects they used every day.

When the family visited London, Mr. Nightingale often took them to visit the British Museum. In the museum were room after room full of objects from Egypt. There were beautiful marble statues. They had been carved centuries earlier. After studying the pharaohs, Florence was excited about making another trip to the museum.

"Papa, can we go back to the Egyptian rooms?" she asked. "And could we see the Elgin Marbles?"

The Elgin Marbles were ancient Greek sculptures, the finest in the world. They came from the Parthenon, a temple on the Acropolis in Athens. Lord Elgin got permission to bring them to England. Now, they were displayed in the British Museum.

Mr. Nightingale smiled. "Of course we will. And someday, I'll take you to Greece and show you the Parthenon."

Thrilled, Florence listened even more carefully than usual. All too soon, the history lesson was over. Then, her father gave her work to do. She was to write an essay in French. Of all the languages she studied, French had become her favorite.

She picked up her best quill pen. As she began to write, her father glanced over her shoulder. His daughter always seemed eager to learn. She had no trouble understanding whatever she heard. And like himself, she enjoyed numbers. But what amazed him most was her memory. It was remarkable.

Mr. Nightingale felt proud of his daughter. "There's no doubt about it," he decided. "Florence is very special."

The Call

lorence was growing up. By this time, she no longer was afraid that she was a monster. But she did become convinced of another thing. The life she was leading did not suit her. It made her miserable. Sometimes, she felt as if she had been born into the wrong family.

Her greatest desire was to be useful. Unfortunately, that seemed an impossible dream. Men and women of wealthy families were not expected to work. Their lives were spent hunting and riding horses. They kept busy visiting each other. Women like her mother were taught to entertain visitors. A successful woman knew how to make her guests feel welcome.

The endless parties at Embley bored Florence. The social season in London was worse. Parthe always looked forward to attending parties. Only Florence dreaded them.

Her future seemed black. Was she to spend her whole life gossiping and drinking tea? What a waste of time! she thought. But then she felt ashamed of herself. The Nightingales had a wonderful life. Instead of always complaining, she should feel lucky. Why was she never satisfied?

As Florence grew older, she seemed to be always quarreling with her mother. Mrs. Nightingale even began to blame her husband for the way Florence behaved. The girl was spoiled, she warned. If only Mr. Nightingale had not taught her useless subjects like Latin, everything would be fine.

Mrs. Nightingale had no difficulties with Parthe. But her younger daughter was a mystery to her. Once, she said jokingly to a friend that the Nightingales were ducks who had given birth to a wild swan.

Of course, the battles with her mother made Florence feel terrible. She hated upsetting her. In a few short years, she would have to be like Mrs. Nightingale. It was expected that she would marry and take care of her husband and children.

On her parents' estate, Florence often visited the tenants who had their homes there. At Lea Hurst, she went around from cottage to cottage. With her she carried food and clothing. These gifts were welcomed because the tenants were poor people. When a baby was born, Florence liked to help the new mother. She cooked and cleaned. If someone got sick, she was pleased to nurse the person.

Helping others caused Florence to forget her troubles at home. It also made her feel useful. But her mother firmly objected. She could not deny that it was customary for women to call on the poor. Taking gifts of soup and jam was a kindness. But that was the limit. A well-brought up girl definitely did not do housework for the poor. She did not lower herself and become a kitchenmaid. As usual, Florence was carrying things to an extreme.

When Florence was sixteen, she had an experience that changed her life. One day, she was alone in her room. Suddenly, she heard a voice. It began speaking to her. She did not tell anyone about the voice. She could only describe it in writing. In her diary, she wrote, "On February 7, 1837, God spoke to me and called me to His service."

From that day, she stopped doubting herself. She was not a monster, as she had once feared. It was only that she was different from Parthe and the other girls. Hearing the voice had convinced her of it. There was a very good reason for her unhappiness. She was to have a special purpose in life. God Himself was going to give her a mission to carry out.

Of course, the voice had not told her exactly what she was supposed to do. But it would be important work. She believed that she would be expected to serve people less fortunate than herself. Perhaps, they would be poor and need money. Maybe, they would be sick. They would turn to her for help.

For the first time in her life, Florence felt content. All she had to do now was be patient. Eventually, God would make the plan clear to her.

The Belle of the Ball

anny Nightingale worried more than ever. Unless Florence began going to parties, she would never find a husband. She must forget her odd ideas. It was time for her to be presented at court.

At first, Florence refused. Then Princess Victoria was crowned queen of England and she changed her mind. She was curious about the new queen, who was only a year older than she was. Meeting her sounded like great fun. To her mother's relief, Florence said she would be presented at the same time as Parthe.

Delighted, Mrs. Nightingale busied herself with preparations. Introducing her daughters into society was no simple task. The Nightingales would give parties in honor of the girls. Of course, many guests would be arriving at Embley. That meant building six more rooms onto the house. And that was not all. The ballroom must be remodeled. New carpet had to be laid throughout the house.

In this major undertaking, Mr. Nightingale's help was required, too. He was skilled at planning improvements for Embley and Lea Hurst. All that winter, he worked on the alterations. His attention was now directed to the work. There was little time for his daughters. Like Florence, he plunged into a task with his whole heart. Everything else was put aside and almost forgotten. One project in which he lost interest was his daughters' lessons. Parthe did not care, but Florence missed the daily schoolwork.

Preparing Embley for guests would take a year. During the remodeling, the family couldn't possibly live there. It would be too uncomfortable. One morning, Mrs. Nightingale suggested they spend the time traveling in Europe.

"We could take the girls to Paris," she said to her husband. "Why don't we introduce them to French society?"

She knew the idea would please Parthe. But she expected Florence to begin arguing. Still, a year touring the Continent was just what she needed. It might help her grow up.

Mr. Nightingale looked up from his drawings. "Maybe you're right," he answered. But he did not sound enthusiastic.

"We could go to Italy," Mrs. Nightingale went on. "I think Florence would enjoy seeing the city where she was born."

Hearing that, Mr. Nightingale began to look more interested. "Oh, it would be nice to visit Florence again. I've missed our good friends there...."

But Mrs. Nightingale did not wait to hear the rest. Already she had run out of the room. She hurried to tell her daughters. Parthe squealed with joy. Florence listened to the news more calmly. But soon even she began to get excited. She realized that now she could see Italy's old Roman ruins.

"How long will we stay in Rome?" she asked her mother. "We must visit the Coliseum."

Mrs. Nightingale and Parthe smiled at each other. As usual, Flo's mind was on history.

Weeks were spent preparing for the trip. New ball gowns were sewn. Trunks were filled with the latest suits and hats. Even the carriage was new, specially designed by Mr. Nightingale himself. He wanted his family to travel in comfort.

Finally, they were ready to depart. The trunks were loaded onto the roof of the carriage. Among the traveling party were two servants and the girls' nanny, Mrs. Gale. On the evening of September 15, 1837, the Nightingale family set off for France.

In Paris, Florence gazed at the sights. She spent hours in museums. But as the months went by, she began to change. She showed signs of becoming interested in dinner parties and dances. Soon she really began to enjoy herself.

Parisian society included an interesting mixture of people. Paris was a place where aristocrats from all over Europe gathered. Florence fit in because she could speak foreign languages so well. And her years of lessons had given her knowledge about many subjects. Suddenly, she was making new friends.

She also attracted quite a few male admirers. The men thought she was charming. As a result, Florence found herself one of the most popular young women in the city. Watching her daughter blossom, Mrs. Nightingale was overjoyed.

From France, the Nightingales moved on to Italy. Florence was eager to see the house where she was born. In Florence, she visited all the famous churches. She went to balls given by the Grand Duke. But best of all, she fell in love with the opera. Every evening, she wanted to attend.

"I've become music mad," she admitted. Her mother only smiled. They no longer fought.

In the 1830s, Italy was ruled by Austria. But many Italians wanted their country to be free. When they fought for independence, they were thrown into prison. Some were even forced to leave Italy. Mr. Nightingale sympathized with the Italian freedom fighters. He became friendly with them. Florence was deeply moved, too. She admired their courage. It was hard not to compare her easy life with theirs.

In September 1838, the Nightingales went to Switzerland. In Geneva, they visited Italian friends who had been forced to flee. They made new friends at the university. Mr. Nightingale liked it so well that he wanted to stay for a long time.

But overnight, their plans changed. The political situation in Europe was growing difficult. Just at this time, Louis Napoleon Bonaparte arrived

in Switzerland. He was Napoleon Bonaparte's nephew. Like his uncle, he wanted to become emperor of France. Now, he was trying to overthrow the French government. The French wanted to arrest him. But Louis had been promised safety The Swiss refused to hand him over.

Reading the newspapers, Mr. Nightingale grew nervous.

"I'm afraid there will be a war," he warned.

Florence peered out the window. Already fear had gripped the city. People were panicky. They expected French soldiers to invade the city. To protect themselves, they began building wooden barricades. Florence heard the sound of pounding hammers.

The next morning, the Nightingales headed back to Paris. In the days ahead, they waited anxiously to see what would happen. Finally, England offered Louis Napoleon Bonaparte a safe place to stay.

Luckily, war was avoided. Before long, social life in Paris was just as busy as ever. Invitations to dinner parties and balls were sent out again.

In the spring of 1839, the Nightingales returned home. Their tour had been a great success.

Inner Struggle

In the meantime, the repairs of Embley were completed. The family moved back. There were luxurious new bedrooms. The drawing room was furnished with thick carpets and new sofas.

A few weeks after their return, Florence and her sister were presented at court. It was Queen Victoria's birthday. She was twenty years old. Curtsying to the queen, Florence could not help feeling awed. Afterwards, there was a splendid ball.

In the weeks that followed, Florence and Parthe attended a round of parties. They were caught up in London's glittering social world. Launching her daughters into high society made Mrs. Nightingale feel very proud. And Florence, too, felt happy and excited. She was a huge success. What more could she want?

Still, she had not forgotten the call she had heard. God had spoken to her two years ago. Suddenly, she began to worry. A special purpose had been planned for her. But possibly, she wasn't worthy after all. In her diary, she scolded herself. "All I do is done to win admiration," she wrote.

Being popular was a big temptation for her. She was rich and pretty. Everybody expected her to lead a life of luxury and pleasure. Then why had God called her to His service, she wondered. Finally, she decided that she was too vain, too proud. From now on, she would be humble. Then, maybe, God would speak to her again.

Florence was delighted when her beloved Aunt Mai invited her to London. She especially liked Aunt Mai's children. Her favorite was the youngest, a boy named Shore.

Florence showed her affection for the children by cooking. It was a special treat when she baked cookies for all of them.

At first, Florence enjoyed herself. Many festivities were planned to celebrate Queen Victoria's marriage to Prince Albert. But Florence had a secret plan. She had made up her mind to study mathematics. When her mother heard about it, she blew up. "What nonsense!" she said. Even worse, Florence's father was displeased.

But luckily, Aunt Mai sided with Florence. A math tutor was hired to teach her. For two happy months, Florence studied math and played with the children.

Then it was time to leave. At Lea Hurst, she felt restless. Soon she was taking care of the sick villagers. Of course, this made her family angry. Mrs. Nightingale scolded. Mr. Nightingale went into the library and shut the door. By now, it had become a battle of wills.

The entire household was suffering. More and more, Florence was ill. Sometimes, she felt jumpy and nervous. Sometimes, she fainted.

Florence knew that her parents expected her to marry. At the parties given back at Embley, she had attracted many men. Any one of them would have been glad to marry her. And yet the life of a wife did not appeal to her.

One night at a dance, she had quarreled with her father. He said, "Your mother tells me that you cook for folks in the village." He sounded shocked.

"Papa, I like to," Florence said. "When they get sick, there's nobody to take care of them."

"Perhaps your mother is right. You spend too much time among the villagers."

This made Florence anxious. "Papa, you won't ask me to stop, will you?"

"It's fine to care about people. But in the future, you must remember who you are."

Florence felt terrible. Even her father was against her. Once again, she began fighting with her mother. Parthe constantly criticized her. At home, life was growing unbearable.

She could not forget the misery she had seen in London. On her way to a ball, she saw poor people from the window of her carriage. Poverty was a big problem everywhere in the 1840s. There were not enough jobs. Wages were low. People were hungry.

In the summer of 1842, Florence met Richard Monckton Milnes. He was a wealthy young politician. He also wrote poetry. Like Florence, he was concerned about the welfare of poor people. Soon, he fell in love with Florence. He proposed marriage.

Richard was one of the most eligible bachelors in England. And he seemed to be perfect for Florence. The marriage was exactly what her parents had always wanted for her. Florence hesitated. She loved and admired Richard. But being a politician's wife would mean the end of her own dreams.

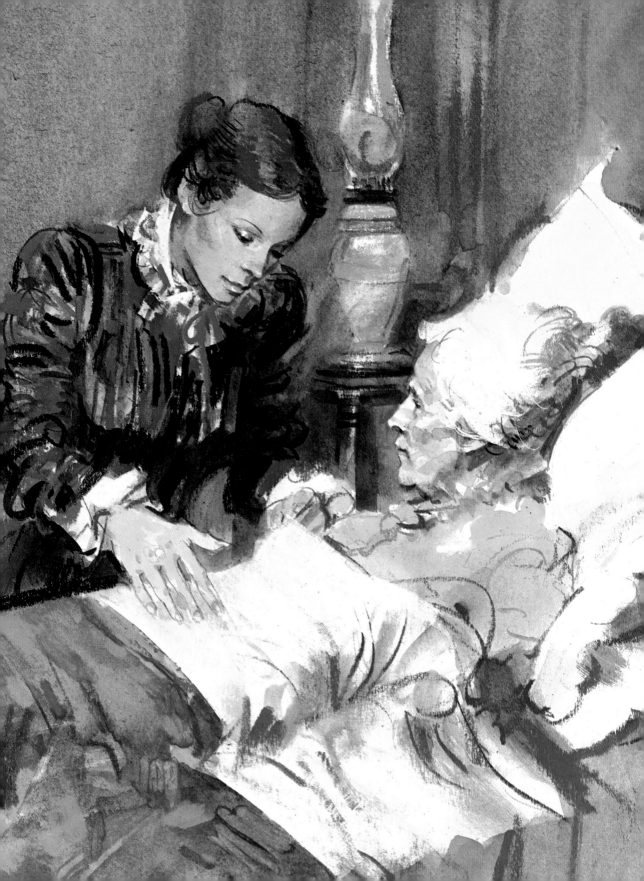

In those days it was out of the question for a married woman to work. If she wed Richard, she would have to devote herself to his career. To the end of her days, she would have to be a society wife.

Still, she loved Richard too much to say no. But she could not tell him yes either. She said that she could not give him a definite answer yet. But he was willing to wait.

At Lea Hurst, that summer, she cared for a poor old woman who lived alone. Each day, she brought food. She rubbed her legs with healing ointments. The woman looked forward to seeing Florence. In the fall, Florence begged to stay at Lea Hurst all winter. The sick needed her.

"What!" exclaimed Mrs. Nightingale. "And miss the social season? Never!"

Gradually, Florence had been coming to an important decision. She believed her mission was to relieve suffering somehow. The real work of her life would not be giving parties. It would be among the poor and the ill.

Only one question remained. Exactly *how* could she achieve her goal? Now, she finally knew the answer. She wanted to work in hospitals where she could care for the sick. Unfortunately, she dared not mention a word of this to her family.

In the summer of 1844, an American doctor was visiting the Nightingales. His name was Samuel Gridley Howe. He was touring Europe with his wife

Julia. Florence liked the kindly doctor. With a pounding heart, she decided to seek his advice. She asked him to meet her in the library before breakfast.

Early the next morning, she raced downstairs. The household was still asleep. "Dr. Howe," she began nervously, "do you think it would be unladylike for me to do works of charity?"

Dr. Howe listened carefully. "It would be highly unusual," he admitted. "But there's nothing unladylike about helping others."

Florence said, "With all my heart I want to work in hospitals, as Catholic nuns do. Would that really be so dreadful?"

Dr. Howe gave her a warm smile. "If you have a vocation for it, then I say 'go forward!'"

Dr. Howe's encouragement gave Florence hope. Now, she felt sure that nursing was the right path for her. Even so, more disappointments lay in store. Summer at Lea Hurst was always her busiest time. But this year, there was an outbreak of scarlet fever in the village. Forbidden to go near the tenants, she spent the summer indoors with nothing to do. She felt useless.

Another year dragged by. Eight years had passed since she heard God's call. By now, she was twenty-five years old. Everything seemed a complete waste of time.

Breaking Away

n 1845, Florence was finally able to prove her nursing skills to her own family. Her grandmother fell ill. Florence nursed her back to health. Then, the Nightingales' faithful old nanny, Mrs. Gale, also became sick and feeble. For many years, she had lived with them. She was one of the family. Tenderly, Florence cared for Mrs. Gale until she died.

In time, the Nightingales began to change their minds. They could no longer deny that Florence had a talent for helping the sick. When she went to visit the villagers, they no longer tried to stop her.

While nursing the local people, Florence made a discovery. To her surprise, she realized that she knew almost nothing about nursing. In those days, it was believed that women were, by nature, best at caring for the sick. Special training was considered unnecessary. But from her experience, Florence found out this was false.

It was clear that a good nurse must know something about medicine. Indeed, that was only the beginning. To become a really fine nurse, she must get practical training at a hospital.

Florence had an idea. A few miles from Embley was a hospital. She decided to study at Salisbury Infirmary. Watching the doctors as they worked would be a good way to learn. But when she mentioned this to the family, they were against it.

"Do you want to disgrace us?" her mother asked angrily. "What will our friends think?"

Parthe shouted, "You might as well go to work as a kitchenmaid." Then, she began to cry.

Mr. Nightingale was too furious to speak. His daughter was not an ordinary woman. She was brilliant. Did she intend to spend her life scrubbing floors in some filthy hospital? Disgusted, he left the parlor without saying a word.

It is not hard to understand why the family was upset. In those times, hospitals were very different from the way they are today. Patients were crowded into filthy wards. Bugs crawled over food. Rats ran between beds. Antiseptics had not been discovered yet, and so hospitals smelled bad.

Nobody went willingly to hospitals. The rich were cared for at home. Poor people went because they had no choice. Conditions were so frightful that nobody wanted to work in hospitals either. That was why nurses were hired from the poorest ranks of society. The women were often too ignorant to work as household servants. Many were drunkards. Or, they began to drink after working in hospitals.

No special training was given to nurses. When they treated patients roughly, nobody told them it was wrong. Seldom did they bother to change the bedding or wash the sick people.

Nurses were outcasts. The nursing profession was not respectable. No wonder the Nightingales were unhappy. They forbid Florence to step foot in Salisbury Infirmary.

But Florence refused to give up. If she could not train inside a hospital, she vowed to study them from outside. Secretly, she began to collect writings about public health. She gathered information from hospitals and from government health officials. Before long, she owned thousands of documents. At night, while her family slept, she read.

In the meantime, Richard Milnes was still waiting for Florence's answer. Seven years had passed. He was growing impatient. Florence loved him. But she knew how miserable she would be as a wife. Unless she could pursue her work, life would have no meaning for her. With a heavy heart, she told Richard she would not marry him.

When Fanny Nightingale heard the news, she was very angry. She accused her daughter of being selfish. Family life became so unpleasant that the strain was beginning to affect Florence's health. She came close to collapse.

Luckily, she had understanding friends. They invited her to join them on a tour of Egypt and Greece. In Athens, she visited the Parthenon. To see the temple after her years of study gave her a thrill.

But it was in Germany that the turning point of her entire life took place. Kaiserwerth was a small village near the Rhine River. There, Florence visited a hospital. Its founder was a Lutheran minister named Theodore Fliedner. He offered to show her around. Opening a door, he said, "And here is where our orphan children sleep."

Florence stared at the children in their beds. She could hardly believe her eyes. They seemed so peaceful and happy. It was nothing like English orphan homes. Pastor Fliedner told her that the hospital always had more patients than it could handle. Several years ago he started a school to train nurses from the Lutheran Church.

Florence asked eagerly, "May I train here?"

Paster Fliedner looked surprised. "Our nurses are simple farm girls from the village. They work from sunrise to sundown. But they are used to scrubbing floors and doing hard work. Do you really wish to live this way?"

"More than anything," she replied.

When she returned home, she told her family of her plan. This time she did not ask their permission. She quietly told them that she intended to train at Kaiserwerth. Immediately, another scene took place.

"Florence, I refuse to discuss this again," her mother said.

Florence argued, "But it's not like English hospitals. Kaiserwerth is clean. And all the nurses are churchwomen."

Her family would not listen to her. Weeks went by. Soon, Florence found herself caught up in the routine of family life at Embley. She felt trapped. Still, she was determined to carry out her plan. This upset Parthe, who loved her sister very much. Each day, she tried to talk her out of going back to Germany.

Florence wanted her family's approval. But over the years, her determination to be a nurse had not weakened. In fact, it had constantly grown stronger. Still, they continued to block her way. Now, she was obliged to defy them. There was no other choice. This would mean breaking away from them. She would have to set out on her own.

In London, Florence Nightingale met an American woman named Elizabeth Blackwell. In the United States, Blackwell had been the first woman to become a doctor. Dr. Blackwell told Florence that she, too, had struggled with her family. They had tried to prevent her from going to medical school.

Elizabeth Blackwell became a model for Florence. Meeting the American woman encouraged her to seek her own dream.

Florence continued to seek her sister's sympathy. She was sorry they bickered so much. It seemed impossible for them to understand each other. Parthe thought that Flo should be satisfied at home. And Florence wanted Parthe's blessing.

One spring day, in 1851, they were sitting in the garden at Embley. It was a perfect afternoon. Parthe

was sketching. Florence was reading a book of poetry. Suddenly, Parthe looked over at her.

"Flo, why are you so set on working in a hospital?" The expression on her face was serious. "Here, you have everything you could desire. What do you really want? What would make you happy?"

"To help other people," Florence said. "It's true that we want for nothing. But Parthe, look around. Everywhere, there is pain and misery."

Possibly, in some small way, she could relieve a little of that pain. Then, she would feel her life had been useful. Only then would she be content.

Florence said to her sister, "After I'm finished training at Kaiserwerth, I'm going to live in London. I'd like to work in a hospital."

"Mother will never agree to that," Parthe said quickly. "Didn't she make you promise never to tell anyone about Kaiserwerth? Oh no, she won't change her mind."

In her heart, Florence knew her sister was right. They looked at each other sadly.

The months she spent in Germany were among the best in her life. She worked until she was exhausted. But never had she felt so full of joy. She wrote to her mother, "I find the deepest interest in everything here, and am so well in body and mind."

And then she added, "Now I know what it is to live and to love life...I wish for no other earth, no other world but this."

Fanny Nightingale must have read those words with deep disappointment. The Nightingales were still hoping for a miracle. Surely the long hours and rough work would bring Florence to her senses. But she seemed more determined than ever.

Mr. Nightingale was a sensible man. Two years later, he accepted defeat. It was clear that his daughter would go her own way. He decided to give her an income to spend as she wished. As an independent woman, she would be free to lead her own life.

Since Florence had first heard the call, sixteen years had passed. At last, it was time to begin her mission.

"There Is But One Person in England"

On August 12, 1853, Florence was chosen for her first nursing job. She was put in charge of a private nursing home in London. During her long struggle with her family, Aunt Mai had always stood by her side. But others also believed in her mission.

Among her friends were people trying their best to improve the way hospitals cared for patients. The most important was Sidney Herbert. As Britain's secretary of war, he was responsible for running the army hospitals. Over the years, Sidney Herbert had come to admire Florence's determination. He respected her great knowledge of hospitals, which she had gained from years of private study.

On November 30, 1853, something happened to change both their lives. The incident took place a continent away. A Turkish fleet in the Crimea was sunk by a Russian ship. The orders to attack were given by Czar Nicholas I.

The czar was determined to make the Russian Navy as powerful as the British and the French Navies. First, he set up a naval base at Sebastopol. This Russian city was located on the tip of the Crimea, a peninsula that extends into the Black Sea.

But the plan did not satisfy the czar. His warships still could not compete with the great fleets of Britain and France. The path leading from the Black Sea to the Mediterranean Sea was through a narrow strip of water that belonged to Turkey. Seeing his ships bottled up, the czar looked for a solution. Finally, he decided to conquer Turkey.

The Turks called on their friends for help. On March 27, 1854, Turkey, France, and Britain declared war on Russia.

The Allies won the first battles. When the news reached home, the British rejoiced. But victory was achieved at a steep price. Many men were killed on the battlefield. Even worse, many other soldiers died of diseases such as cholera.

William H. Russell was a reporter for the *London Times*. He was one of the first newspaper reporters to ever describe a war. The reports he sent back from the Crimea were unbelievable. The British Army was badly organized, Russell wrote. In the army hospitals, the wounded got poor care. There were almost no medical supplies to treat the sick. The suffering of the soldiers was shocking. The truth was that hundreds of men had died needlessly.

Russell's reports had an immediate effect. People were outraged when they learned the facts. Something had to be done. The *Times* began to collect money for medical supplies. Donations poured in from all over the country. People were asking the government to explain what had gone wrong. Much of the criticism fell on Florence's friend, Sidney Herbert.

The first step was to find out how bad the crisis really was. The British Army had a hospital near the Turkish village of Scutari. Sidney Herbert decided to send a committee to Turkey. He needed the right person to lead the group and get the facts for him. Ideally, the person should be well informed about how to organize hospitals. There was no doubt in his mind about the one person who could do this mission best. She was Florence Nightingale.

In October 1854, Sidney Herbert asked Florence to take a group of nurses to Scutari. Until now, nurses had never been allowed to work in army hospitals. But this time was different. There was a desperate need for skilled people. Nothing else mattered.

Writing to Florence, Sidney Herbert said, "There is but one person in England that I know of who would be capable of organizing and superintending such a scheme...."

In this historic letter, he warned that the nurses would face a terrible task. They had no idea how horrible war could be. They would need great courage and great energy. But if they agreed to go, it would show what women could do.

His idea did not take Florence by surprise. Even before Sidney Herbert's letter arrived, she herself had written to him. She offered her services, saying that she was eager to go to the Crimea. Their letters crossed in the mail.

When her family heard about Sidney Herbert's offer, they could not believe it.

To be chosen for this job was a great honor. It was the first time a woman had been picked to officially represent the British government. The news caused a stir throughout the country.

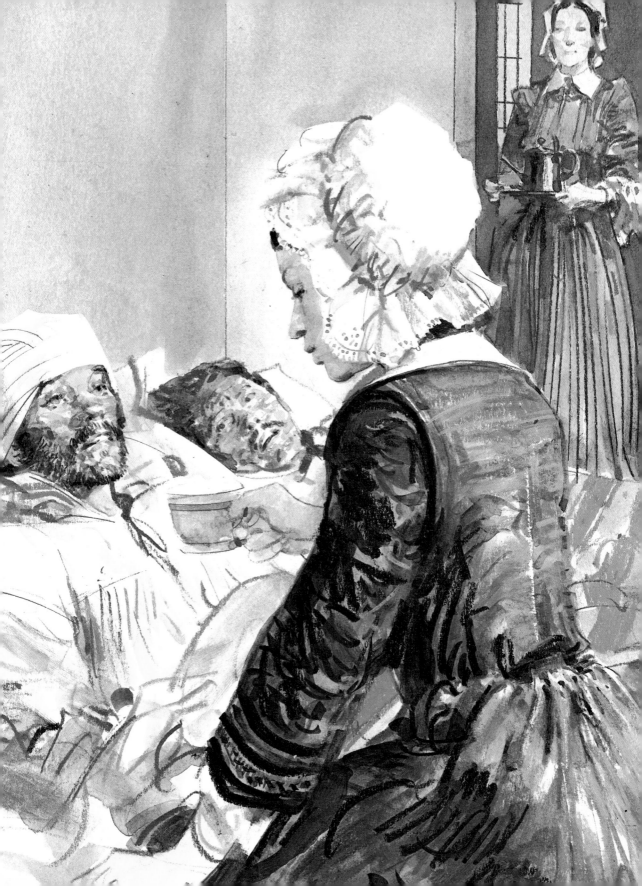

But Florence took the appointment calmly. There was much to do before she could leave. She had to quickly find nurses willing to accompany her. It would not be easy. But she knew that this would be an important test for women. If they met the challenge, nurses should never again be treated with contempt. It would mean a huge leap forward.

On October 21, 1854, she sailed to Constantinople with thirty-eight nurses. As they arrived, she could see Scutari from the deck of the ship. The hospital was a large building. At one time, it had been an army barracks where Turkish soldiers lived. The British had turned the place into an emergency hospital for its wounded. The building had been quickly painted. Otherwise, no thought had been given to cleanliness.

Nothing she had read in the papers had prepared Florence for Scutari. The hospital was stinking and filthy. Underneath the building flowed an open sewer. It had never been drained. Through the pipes, the stench rose up into the wards.

Worse, there were nearly four miles of patients in the hospital. A lucky few had beds. The rest lay on the floor or on straw mattresses. They were tormented by rats and insects.

Florence saw men with no blankets to cover them. For days, they shivered half naked, waiting for treatment. And there was practically nothing to eat. Each day the sick soldiers received a small piece of boiled meat. But they got no knives or forks. The men had to tear apart the meat with their fingers. Some were too weak to feed themselves. To these men went the thin broth left over in the pot after the meat had been boiled.

Some of the army doctors resented Florence. They thought she would hinder their work. At first, they tried to stop her from nursing the patients.

But then disaster struck. There was a terrible battle at Balaclava. A brigade of British soldiers on horses got their orders confused. They charged right into the Russian guns and were butchered. On top of this mistake, an epidemic of cholera broke out. Thousands of soldiers became ill with the disease.

Winter arrived in the Crimea. Fierce winds began to howl. Throughout those icy months, the city of Sebastopol was crowded with British soldiers. They froze because of the bitter cold. A supply ship bringing food and clothing to the army sunk during a hurricane. There was not enough medicine. Healthy men began to grow ill. They, too, were shipped across the Black Sea to join the wounded soldiers at Scutari.

Soon there were more soldiers in the hospital than fighting at the front. The doctors were unable to care for everyone. Desperate, they finally accepted Florence's help.

The women went to work. To make more beds, they began stuffing cloth with straw. The kitchen staff was told to cook nourishing soups and puddings.

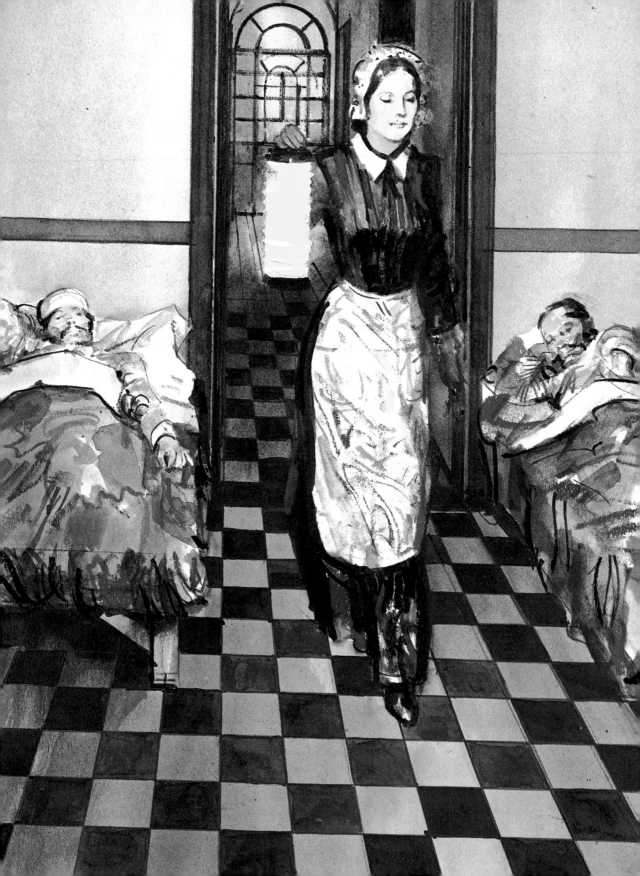

Florence told her nurses to wash the men before attending to their wounds. But some of the wounded men would not allow the women to come near them. Covered with filth, they felt disgusting. Even their own mothers would not touch them now, they argued.

But Florence insisted. "We've seen lots of bad things here," she told them. "We have strong stomachs."

She knew that it was important to win the respect of the doctors. She had to convince them that she was there to help, not to interfere. "Remember," she kept reminding her nurses, "Whenever a doctor gives an order, be sure and follow it."

Before long, Florence had won the love of her patients. Each evening, she checked on the men before going to bed. Carrying a lamp, she walked through the wards. She always seemed to know which men were the most seriously ill.

Two thousand patients died at Scutari. Often, it was Florence who sat at their bedsides. It was Florence who held their hands. She wrote down their last words and sent letters to their families. To the dying men, Florence seemed like a saint.

The Lady With the Lamp

lorence was working almost round-the-clock to care for the soldiers. Her entire life, she had been fiercely devoted to people she cared about. Now, she gave her love and tenderness to the wounded.

Since she was a young girl, her biggest fault had been her stubbornness. But at Scutari, this trait turned out to be useful. The conditions there could not have been more discouraging. A wishy-washy person would not have lasted long.

The years of up-and-down struggle with her family had turned her into a strong person. Other traits in her character also came in handy. Always outspoken, her calm and open manner impressed everyone at the hospital. Her ability to control herself made her a natural leader. And her talent for math made her an extremely good organizer.

Day by day, conditions in the hospital improved slightly. But it was a struggle. Before leaving England, Florence was told that the soldiers had everything they needed. Still, she had taken the precaution of bringing along a stock of supplies. Of course, she used her own money to purchase them.

Arriving in the Crimea, she quickly learned the truth. The soldiers needed a great many things. She distributed clothing and bedding and eating utensils. And when she ran out, she ordered more. Before long, the whole hospital was depending on her for supplies.

A man from the *London Times* came to visit the hospital. The paper had gathered a large amount of money for medical supplies. But officials were insisting that the hospitals didn't need any money. They suggested the *Times* build a church instead. When Florence heard about this, she was angry, but not suprised.

Many times she had asked the government to visit and see conditions for themselves. The hospital was always short of supplies. The problem was red tape. There were so many rules and regulations about sending things to the army. It seemed like dozens of useless forms had to be filled out. As a result, shiploads of food rotted in the harbor. In the meantime, her patients were starving. It made her furious.

Much to her joy, the *Times* offered her its fund. Eagerly, she and her nurses hurried to the large markets at Constantinople. There, they bought fifty thousand shirts for the patients. Over the next months, they purchased towels, sheets, socks, and many other necessary items.

By December, another crisis had struck. Florence got word that five hundred new patients would be arriving soon. Unfortunately, there was no room for them. She had an idea. One of the hospital wings had been destroyed by fire. If it were rebuilt, there could be room for a thousand men. Her suggestion to rebuild was not well received.

"It would take at least a year," an official said.

"But the men will be here next month!" she exclaimed.

Florence refused to take no for an answer. She was determined to rebuild the wing. Finally, she persuaded the British ambassador to give her money. Then she hired Turkish workmen.

But bad luck hounded her. The workmen went on strike. Then, the ambassador changed his mind about the money.

Still determined, she went ahead and hired more workmen—two hundred of them. This time, she paid their wages out of her own pocket. When the new patients finally arrived, work on the burned wing was finished.

It was not unusual for Florence to work sixteen or twenty hours a day. Her energy seemed incredible. But after several months, she began to feel exhausted. Refusing to rest, she got sick. Aunt Mai left her husband and children at home and came to take care of Florence.

Florence and her aunt shared a room about the size of a closet. There was only space for two beds and a table. She used the table as a writing desk.

The men running the hospital had set aside only six rooms for all the nurses. They hoped the women would get discouraged and leave. But Florence had arranged the rooms into cozy quarters for her staff.

All day long, she nursed patients. Late in the evening, she sat at her desk. By the light of a candle, she would compose letters. She wrote to thousands of families whose sons had died. And to Sidney Herbert she wrote long reports, describing her work. She also made many suggestions on how to improve the conditions at the hospital.

It was not unusual for Florence to work through the night. Then, at dawn, she would throw herself on the bed and try to get a few hours of sleep.

One night, Aunt Mai said, "Flo, let me help with that letter. You haven't slept more than three hours any night this week."

"Thank you," she replied. "But this one I must do myself."

She was writing to Sidney Herbert. There was much to tell. Queen Victoria herself had become interested in the hospital. Now, there were places where the recovered soldiers could relax before going back to battle. There were books to read. They could gather with their friends for a cup of tea.

Before this, there had been no place to meet
except bars. The men would spend their free time
drinking. There was nothing else to do. It was not
surprising that some drank up most of their army
pay. Their families back in England saw little of it.

But when they did send money home, often it
never reached their relatives. When Florence heard
about it, she felt concerned. She collected the men's
pay and sent it herself. Finally, she wrote Queen
Victoria, asking for special post offices for soldiers.

The queen was one of her biggest admirers. In
December 1855, Victoria wrote to praise Florence's
work. The queen also told Florence that she dearly
wished to send the soldiers some kind of gift.

Writing back, Florence said the best gift would
be a fairer system of paying the army. When soldiers
fell ill and could not fight, they received smaller
wages than soldiers wounded in battle. Florence
thought this was terribly wrong. Queen Victoria
agreed. Several months later, the system was
changed. All soldiers were paid equally.

Six months passed quickly. At the hospital,
soldiers were getting healthy food to eat. They had
clean clothes and fresh sheets. The hospital wards
were scrubbed. Each patient had a bed.

In the 1850's, merciful drugs to kill pain were
not available. Doctors operated on patients without
chloroform. Often, the soldiers had these operations
right on their beds. The patients lying nearby could

not help seeing and hearing. Florence bought screens. She set them up around the beds. She also introduced special tables for use in operations.

One of the worst conditions was the sewer under the hospital. Florence managed to have it drained and disinfected. Once this was done, the death rate tumbled by eighty percent.

In the wards, patients with infectious diseases lay next to men with battle wounds. Florence decided to place them in separate wards. Separating them decreased the number of dead still further.

The improvements taking place at Scutari were incredible. Everyone knew that Florence was responsible. During the long winter of 1855, she became a symbol of hope for the soldiers. Their spirits rose. Maybe they would survive the terrible war after all. The sound of laughter began to be heard again. Recovering their sense of humor, the men organized singing groups. They played chess and dominoes. The most healthy patients played games out-of-doors.

It was no wonder that the soldiers began to call Florence the Angel of the Crimea. At night, they waited for the sight of her shining lantern. Hearing her speak was a comfort. Some patients actually kissed her shadow.

In England, the name Florence Nightingale became a household word. Songs were written about her. Patients named their baby girls after her. Racehorses and ships also were christened Florence.

Suddenly, she was one of the most famous women in the world. The public was eager to know everything about her. No detail about her work in the Crimea was too small to report. The story of her heroic life was hastily published. These little leaflets sold on the street for a penny. Newspapers rushed to cash in. They published many stories describing her life of sacrifice.

Not content to just read about Florence, people also wanted to see what she looked like. They bought colored pictures of her to hang on their walls. And in the streets of London, peddlers were busy selling Florence Nightingale statues.

Her overnight popularity delighted the Nightingale family. After many years of fighting against her, they were now completely won over. Letters praising Florence poured into Embley. Parthe took on the task of answering all of the fan mail her sister received.

The only person not excited about all of this new popularity was Florence herself. Fame could not have interested her less. She had no time to waste on personal glory, she declared. In the Crimea, soldiers were still dying. There was still much more work to be done.

Home Again

he spring of 1855 was a difficult time. By now conditions at Scutari had improved greatly. Florence decided to visit other hospitals located near the battlefields. On May 5, she crossed the Black Sea to the war front, at Sebastopol. Along the way, soldiers cheered and presented bouquets of flowers.

But doctors at the field hospitals did not welcome her. It was the same story as at Scutari when she had first arrived. She was accused of meddling and causing trouble. Florence ignored the medical officers. Stubbornly, she traveled from hospital to hospital on horseback.

Freezing rainstorms lashed the Crimea. Chilled and exhausted, Florence collapsed. She became seriously ill with Crimean fever. Already run down from months of overwork, doctors expected her to die. At Scutari, soldiers wept. When the news reached England, people were shocked with grief.

But two weeks later, she slowly began to get well. A cable was sent to Queen Victoria announcing the good news. There was much rejoicing over Florence's recovery. A fund was set up to support her work. Money flooded in from admirers all over the country. Later, the Nightingale Fund would be used to start the first school to train nurses.

In the fall, the war was coming to an end. The British seized the Russian base at Sebastopol. In the next months, there were fewer patients at Scutari. On March 30, 1856, the peace treaty was signed. At that time, all of the sick soldiers were sent home. The last patient left the hospital on July 16.

Several weeks later, the Nightingales were sitting in their parlor at Lea Hurst. Suddenly, they heard a shriek. The housekeeper was staring at someone outside the window.

"It's Miss Florence!" she cried.

A special welcome had been planned for the Lady with the Lamp. In London, army bands were waiting to greet her. But Florence slipped quietly into England. Wanting no speeches and parades, she had traveled from Constantinople under the name of "Miss Smith." Nobody knew who she was.

Leaving the ship, she arrived in London. Still, she escaped people's notice. Then she had caught a train to Lea Hurst and walked home. The family was taken completely by surprise.

The Nightingales had not seen Florence for two years. Her mother was shocked to see how thin she had grown. She looked tired and ill.

"You must rest," Mrs. Nightingale urged her daughter. "The war has worn you out. Now you deserve a long rest."

"But I don't have time to rest," Florence replied. She knew that people in England loved and trusted her. Now they might pay attention to her views on public health. The war was still fresh in everybody's mind. This was the time to fight for even more changes.

At Scutari, she had begun to think of patients as her own family. Thousands of her "children" had died in the Crimea from disease and poor care, not from their wounds. Soon, they would be forgotten. "But I can never forget!" she wrote. She vowed this would never happen again.

Florence was now thirty-six years old. She was a famous woman. People wanted to meet her. She was in demand at dinners and receptions. But she shunned these social events.

Better than anyone, she knew how poor her own health really had become. Sometimes, she felt that she might not live very long. Perhaps there would be only a few years to complete her mission. So she threw herself into stirring up the country. The army's medical service must be reformed.

Queen Victoria invited her to Scotland. The two women sat and talked. Scutari had touched the queen's heart. She wanted to hear about Florence's experiences from her own lips. At Balmoral Castle, Florence decribed the terrible events she had seen.

Then, she took advantage of the private meeting to suggest a plan. Improvements in the army medical service were desperately needed. She pleaded with Queen Victoria to set up a royal commission to

examine medical service conditions. Often, disease could be prevented in both times of war and peace, she said. If soldiers were in good health, England would not have to again suffer a horror as bad as the Crimean War had been.

The queen listened. Afterwards, she exclaimed to her ministers, "What a head! I wish we had her at the war office."

Victoria agreed to form a royal commission. The most logical person to lead the group was Florence. But in those days women were not allowed to take such positions. Even the queen herself could not change tradition easily. So Sidney Herbert was chosen to head the group instead. But it was Florence who did most of the work. She pointed out the problems. And it was Florence who came up with the answers, too.

Eventually, the royal commission presented its report. Many of Florence's suggestions were then put into use.

One of her oldest dreams was a school for nurses. By now the Nightingale Fund had grown to several hundred thousand dollars. This was more than enough to get started. The school was set up at St. Thomas's Hospital in London. The students would live there. Doctors on the staff would give them thorough training. From that moment on, a new age had dawned for nursing—and for patients as well.

The Nightingale School

O n July 9, 1860, the Nightingale School opened. For the first time in history, people could learn how to nurse by attending school. Until now, the only ones to receive training had been nuns or other religious women.

Fifteen young women were in the first class. They had been chosen with care. Florence's standards were high. She insisted the students come from good families. Strict rules of behavior were laid down.

She stressed that they were pioneers. Despite all her work at Scutari, most people still had a low

opinion of most nurses. They continued to picture nurses as ignorant. And their reputation as drunks still clung.

Florence knew she had to change those opinions. It was important to prove that nurses had the ability to take charge of patients' health. Like doctors, nurses practiced a profession. They deserved respect.

All of the women were interviewed by Florence. Only then were they invited to study at the school. Afterwards, Florence continued to keep an eye on them. The training program lasted one year. She paid close attention to the women's progress.

When the school first opened, the class came to visit Florence at her home in London. They could hardly wait to begin classes. Florence liked their enthusiasm. The women who gathered in her parlor were all dressed alike. They wore plain brown dresses topped by neat white aprons. On their heads perched clean white caps.

Florence had designed the uniforms herself. Having the women wear special clothing was another of her new ideas. Before that time, nurses had always worked in ordinary clothes.

It did not take the students long to start asking questions. All of them looked forward to working with patients.

"Miss Nightingale," one student asked, "when will we be able to care for patients on our own?"

Florence smiled. She understood their impatience. "Not until the end of the year, I'm afraid," she answered. "But in the meantime you'll have a great deal to keep you busy."

Then she began to describe their daily routine. Each morning, they must be in the hospital wards by seven A.M. Patients had to be washed, fed, and given medicines. Until lunchtime, the women would learn by practical experience.

In the afternoon, there would be a lecture. The teacher would be one of the doctors at St. Thomas's Hospital. Afterwards, they would return to the wards and give patients their suppers. At nine o'clock, their duties would be finished.

But their day was not over yet. "Then," Florence added, "you must write up your lecture notes. The head nurse and I will look them over."

Someone asked, "When can we assist the doctors in operations?"

"Not until you've heard several lectures on the correct way to treat a certain disease. Then, you'll be ready to help the doctors."

Later on, Florence wrote a popular book on nursing. *Notes on Nursing* was a practical book for nurses. Full of her usual good sense, Florence insisted on fresh air, cleanliness, and wholesome food for patients. Another book was called *Notes on Hospitals*. By this time, she was an expert on the best way to build and run a hospital.

The Final Years

lorence became seriously ill. Years of overwork had wrecked her health. An invalid, she spent most of her time in bed. Seldom did she ever leave her London house. Good friends and Aunt Mai looked after her.

Even so, she kept on working just as hard as ever. The Nightingale School became a huge success. Florence was its guiding spirit. But no longer did she have the physical strength to run the school. Instead, she put in charge a trusted head nurse named Mrs. Wardroper.

A great number of nurses completed the course. They went on to work at hospitals in many lands. Some of the graduates later founded nursing schools of their own. One of these was the first nursing school in the United States. It was set up at Bellevue Hospital, in New York City. So Florence Nightingale's ideas about nursing continued to spread all over the world.

From her bed, Florence helped others, whenever she could. At this time, the Civil War was being fought in the United States. President Lincoln's secretary of war asked for advice about setting up hospitals for the Union Army. The govenment remembered her work in the Crimea. For the first time, American women were being allowed to nurse the soldiers. But they needed practical advice.

Throughout the Civil War, Florence exchanged letters with Dorothea Dix. Miss Dix was the superintendent of nurses in Washington, D.C. In the end, thousands of Union soldiers owed their lives to Florence.

Both in England and abroad, she became the mastermind behind many reforms in medicine. At that time, India was not an independent country. It was still a colony in the British Empire. Many English soldiers and their families lived there.

In India, ideas on sanitation were still backward. Many people did not use good hygiene. And their diet was poor, too. As a result, many people who lived there suffered from illnesses. It was common for poor people to die young.

Aware of the need for better health conditions in India, Florence urged that a special study should be made. A royal commission was set up. Once again, Florence worked behind the scenes. Her practical suggestions improved the health of both the British soldiers stationed in the colony and the Indian people.

In 1897, Victoria had been queen for sixty years. There was a grand celebration, called the Diamond Jubilee. Special programs were organized to recall the important events of her reign. One of them was an exhibition on nursing. As a result of this exhibition, Florence won great praise as the pioneer of modern nursing. Once again, her popularity soared among the citizens of England.

During these years she was surrounded by a loving family—people like her Aunt Mai and her cousin Shore. She was very fond of them.

As a new century began, Florence continued to receive public honors. In 1907, Britain gave her the Order of Merit. She was the first woman ever to receive this award. Henry Dunant, founder of the International Red Cross, also paid tribute to her. He said that Florence's work in the Crimea had inspired him to begin the Red Cross.

In old age, she put on weight and grew stout. Her eyesight grew weaker and weaker. She became blind in 1901. Now, she was forced to slow down. But her work had been completed. She had succeeded in changing the image of nurses. The public now saw them as professionals who were dedicated to healing the sick.

For the last ten years of her life, Florence was cut off from the outside world. Her sight was completely gone. She was always ailing. Most of the friends she really cared about were dead. Even Queen Victoria had died.

On August 13, 1910, she died peacefully, at the age of ninety.

The American Civil War

During the four years of the Civil War, 618,000 men died. More Americans perished during the Civil War than in all of America's other wars combined. Of that number, over half died of sickness and disease rather than on the battlefield. Hundreds of thousands perished needlessly because of the inadequate medical care available to the soldiers and the unsanitary conditions in the army camps. Seven out of every ten deaths in the Union Army were caused by disease, while in the Confederate Army, where conditions were even worse, three out of every four deaths resulted from disease. Medical treatment was so poor that the chances of surviving a wound were only seven to one.

The northern states quickly realized the need for proper medical care for their soldiers. They turned to Florence Nightingale for help in October 1861, seven months after the start of the Civil War. At President Lincoln's request, the secretary of war urgently asked for her advice on organizing the hospitals of the Union Army. On October 8, Florence Nightingale sent the secretary all the statistical reports she had gathered on the Crimea. Throughout the war, she corresponded with Dorothea Dix, the superintendent of nurses in Washington, D.C. Florence Nightingale gave Dix guidelines for setting up proper medical treatment for the Union soldiers. Following Nightingale's example in the Crimea, female nurses were introduced into the army hospitals. Also, care was taken to give sick soldiers a nourishing diet. A Sanitary Commission was appointed to investigate the conditions of the army hospitals.

Florence Nightingale would willingly have advised the Confederates as well. She wrote that she was "horrified at the reports of the sufferings of their wounded." However, the southern army never contacted her.

Despite the improvements in health care for Union soldiers—thanks to Florence Nightingale's advice—thousands of northern soldiers died because of the primitive medical treatment then available. Her work in the Crimea was quoted in Union medical journals. It changed future American health care systems. When the war ended in 1865, the secretary of the United States Christian Union thanked Florence Nightingale for her help, writing: "Your influence and our indebtedness to you can never be known."

Fredericksburg, Virginia, after the
Battle of Fredericksburg—Civil War photograph

Soldiers wounded at the Battle of
Fredericksburg—Civil War photograph

Clara Barton, Henri Dunant, and the International Red Cross

Clara Barton was the first woman clerk in the U.S. Patent Office. After the outbreak of the Civil War in 1861, she served as a nurse, caring for wounded men on the battlefield. She also established a system for providing supplies to the soldiers in the camps. Her work attracted national attention. Called the Angel of the Battlefield, she was appointed by President Lincoln in 1865 to search for missing soldiers. Clara Barton eventually tracked down thousands of men whose fate after the war had been unknown, including 12,000 Union soldiers buried in unmarked graves near the prison of Andersonville in Georgia.

In 1869, Clara Barton served as a nurse during the Franco-Prussian War. There she observed the work of the International Red Cross, founded by Jean Henri Dunant, a Swiss banker. Dunant had been shocked when he accidentally saw the poor medical care given wounded soldiers at the battle of Solferino in 1859. Condemning this lack of adequate treatment, he wrote a book titled *Recollections of Solferino*. In it, he suggested that an international society of volunteers be created to care for sick and wounded soldiers in time of war. Impressed by his idea, several European nations agreed to his proposal. The International Red Cross was established in 1863 and was put into practice the following year during the Geneva Convention. While he

Clara Barton, founder of the American Red Cross

was on a visit to London in 1872, Dunant said: "It is to an Englishwoman that all of the honor of that convention is due. What inspired me was the work of Miss Florence Nightingale in the Crimea."

Admiring Dunant's volunteer society, Clara Barton organized the American Red Cross in 1881, after her return to the United States. She headed it until 1904. She was the first person to introduce the idea that the Red Cross should also provide disaster relief during peacetime. Treating victims of earthquakes, epidemics, and other natural disasters has since become one of the main services of the Red Cross.

The Discovery of Anesthetics

Before the mid-nineteenth century, surgery was performed without anesthetics. On the battlefield, wounded soldiers were operated on for their sword and bullet wounds without any substance to relieve their pain. Often the soldiers found their operations as painful as their wounds. Because army hospitals usually didn't have separate operating rooms, soldiers underwent amputations and other difficult surgery on their own beds. The operations were often in full view of the other soldiers. Witnessing these horrible scenes made the other patients even more afraid when it came time for their own operations.

The discovery of anesthetics allowed doctors to perform serious surgery without causing additional pain to patients. Laughing gas, ether, and chloroform anesthetized patients so they would not feel the pain of an operation.

In 1772, the discoverer of oxygen, Joseph Priestly, discovered another gas—nitrous oxide. Seven years later, a fellow English scientist, Humphry Davy, dubbed it "laughing gas" because he found that it produced a state of giddy happiness when it was breathed in. The gas soon became popular, especially in America, where quacks showed its euphoric effects to the public in traveling road shows. One of these was Sam Colt, the inventor of the Colt revolver, the first practical revolving firearm. In a public experiment, he gave laughing gas to a group of Indians to make them dance and raise frenzied war yells. Instead of growing giddy, the Indians fell to the ground, in a deep sleep. This revealed that the gas had not only a euphoric but a lethargic effect—it could make people fall asleep. A third important property of laughing gas was discovered by an American dentist named Horace Wells. In 1844 he attended another public experiment of the gas, given by the showman Gardner Quincy Colton. Pain was inflicted on one of the subjects of the experiment. After breathing in nitrous oxide, the subject seemed insensitive to the pain. Dr. Wells immediately realized the importance of this experiment. To test if the gas did indeed deaden pain, he had one of his own teeth extracted while under the influence of the gas. After the extraction proved painless, nitrous oxide became commonly used in dental surgery from 1846 on.

The following year, a Scottish doctor, James Y. Simpson, tried to find an anesthetic less harmful than ether, which was currently in use. Dr. Simpson and his assistants experimented with chloroform, a clear liquid with a sweet taste and odor. It had been discovered in 1831, but Simpson was the first to give it to patients for the relief of pain. The use of chloroform in medical operations was controversial at first. It became popular for medical operations after Queen Victoria agreed to take it, in 1853, when she gave birth to her eighth child, Prince Leopold. Soon afterwards, anesthetics were widely used in civilian and military hospitals for all types of surgery.

Queen Victoria's Diamond Jubilee

In 1897, Queen Victoria celebrated her sixtieth anniversary on the throne. Part of the Diamond Jubilee festivities included a history of the progress of trained nursing during her reign. It was featured in the Victorian Era Exhibition, which was a retrospective of the cultural developments in Great Britain while Victoria was queen.

Florence Nightingale was the centerpiece of the exhibit on nursing. Its organizers asked her for her souvenirs from Scutari and from the Crimea. She stubbornly refused. All her life she had hated personal publicity. Indignantly, she wrote: "Oh, the absurdity of people and their vulgarity! The relics, the representations of the Crimean War! What are they?

Portrait of Queen Victoria when she was young, painted by the artist A. E. Peuley (Victoria and Albert Museum, London)

They are first the tremendous lessons we have had to learn from its tremendous blunders and ignorances. And next they are Trained Nurses and the progress of Hygiene. These are the 'representations' of the Crimean War. And I will not give my foolish portrait (which I have not got) or anything else as 'relics' of the Crimea. It is too ridiculous." Nevertheless, the organizers finally pressured her into giving a bust of herself. They also discovered her Crimean traveling carriage in a farmhouse at Embley.

Florence Nightingale was a great favorite of Queen Victoria. Although Florence continued to do important work in health care reform for forty years after her experiences in the Crimea, only the queen and a few members of the government were aware of it. Because of her seclusion, the general public believed Florence was dead. The exhibit made her a popular figure in England once more. Old veterans of the Crimea wept when they saw her carriage and went up to kiss it. One admirer left fresh flowers daily beneath her statue. Only Florence Nightingale herself was not pleased with all this adoration, because she considered that the true benefit of the Crimean War was not her fame but the advances in nursing and proper medical care.

HISTORICAL CHRONOLOGY

Florence Nightingale's Life	Historical and Cultural Events
	1819 May 24—Princess Victoria is born in England.
1820 May 12—Florence Nightingale is born in Florence, Italy.	**1820** James Monroe is reelected to his second term as the fifth President of the United States.
1837 February 7— Florence hears the voice of God, calling her to His service. September 8—The Nightingales leave for a tour of Europe. .	**1837** June 20—Princess Victoria becomes Queen of England.
1839 May 24—Florence and her sister, Parthenope, are presented at court · on Queen Victoria's twentieth birthday.	

The Return of Rip Van Winkle—John Quidor
(Andrew Mellon Collection, National Gallery of Art)

Florence Nightingale's Life	Historical and Cultural Events
1840 April-May—Florence studies math and takes care of her Aunt Mai's children in London.	**1840** February 10—Queen Victoria marries Prince Albert. There are celebrations in London and throughout Great Britain.
1844 June—Dr. Samuel Gridley Howe advises Florence to pursue her vocation.	**1844** The Young Men's Christian Association (YMCA) is founded in England.
1851 July-October—Working at a hospital in Kaiserswerth, in Germany, convinces Florence she wants to be a nurse.	**1851** Mary Carpenter sets up schools for the poor children in England. She also founds the first reformatory schools for juvenile delinquents.

(Top) "Red Penny" stamp, one of the first stamps issued in England, depicting Queen Victoria

(Bottom) Five Cent Stamp used in U.S in 1847

James Monroe—the fifth President of the United States

Crimean War fortificatons

Florence Nightingale's Life	Historical and Cultural Events
1853 August 12—Florence is appointed superintendent of a nursing home in London.	**1853** November 30—A Turkish fleet is sunk under orders from Czar Nicholas I.
1854 October 15—Sidney Herbert appoints Florence as head of a commission to investigate medical care in the Crimea. October 21—Leading a party of thirty-eight nurses, Florence sets sail for Turkey, arriving in Constantinople on November 4. From there she goes to Scutari, the British army hospital base. December 14—Queen Victoria writes Florence, praising her work. She asks advice about gifts for the ill soldiers. Florence suggests that salaries be made equal to those of soldiers wounded in battle.	**1854** March 27—In an alliance with Turkey, Britain and France declare war on Russia. September 14—British and French troops land in the Crimea. September 20—The allies win a major victory at the Battle of the Alma. Two thousand men die, thousands more are wounded. A cholera epidemic breaks out, killing many more troops. October 25—The Allied forces again win at the battle of Balaclava, despite a disastrous charge by the light cavalry brigade, which lost half its men.

Florence Nightingale's Life	Historical and Cultural Events
	November 5—The Battle of Inkerman, fought in heavy fog, is another Allied victory, despite heavy losses. November 14—The worst hurricane in Crimean history sinks the British supply ship, the *Prince*.
1855 February 1—The queen puts into effect Florence's proposal. Pay scales are made equal for wounded and sick soldiers.	**1855** September 8— British troops seize the Russian naval base at Sebastopol, virtually ending the war.

Representatives to the treaty negotiations marking the end of the Crimean War—1856

The landing of the Allies at Balaclava (Naval Museum, Genoa, Italy)

Napoleon III, emperor of France—painting by Hippolyte Flandrin

Florence Nightingale's Life	Historical and Cultural Events
May 5—Florence Nightingale travels to the Crimea to investigate hospitals at the front. She falls ill from Crimean fever and is near death for two weeks. May 24—A cable is sent to Queen Victoria informing her that Florence is recovering from her illness. There is national rejoicing in England. The Nightingale Fund, to begin a nursing school, is set up in her honor.	
1856 August 7—Florence returns to England. She is a national heroine but she refuses to be brought home in state.	**1856** March 30—A peace treaty between the Allied forces and Russia is signed in Paris. April-July—The British and French forces return home. The last patient leaves the base hospital at Scutari on July 16.

Florence Nightingale's Life	Historical and Cultural Events
1859 Her two classic works, *Notes on Hospitals* and *Notes on Nursing,* are published.	**1859** The royal commission on the army medical system officially reports its findings to the British government. All of its proposed reforms, drafted by Florence Nightingale, are put into action.
1860 July 9—The Nightingale School opens. This historic date marks the beginning of modern trained nursing.	**1860** Abraham Lincoln is elected sixteenth President of the United States. South Carolina secedes from the Union in protest.

The photographer Nadar took the first aerial photograph from this balloon in 1858

John Brown Going to his Hanging—Horace Pippin (Philadelphia Academy of Fine Arts)

Florence Nightingale's Life	Historical and Cultural Events
1861- **1865** October 1861—The United States secretary of war asks Florence Nightingale for advice on setting up military hospitals for the Union Army. Her suggestions are adopted throughout the Civil War.	**1861-** **1865** The American Civil War cost 618,000 men their lives— more casualties than in all other American wars combined. The majority die from diseases and untreated wounds rather than in battle. Nurses and relief organizations, such as the YMCA, attend the soldiers in the field hospitals.

Abraham Lincoln visits the troops on the Potomac

Florence Nightingale's Life	Historical and Cultural Events
1897 A retrospective on the progress of nursing during Queen Victoria's reign is featured at the Diamond Jubilee celebration. It makes Florence Nightingale a popular figure again in Britain.	**1897** Queen Victoria celebrates her Diamond Jubilee, marking sixty years of her reign as Queen of England.
1901 Henri Dunant, the founder of the Red Cross, receives the Nobel Peace Prize. His work is inspired by Florence Nightingale's experiences in the Crimea.	**1901** January 22—Queen Victoria dies.

Union and Confederate troops clash near Richmond (Biblioteque Nationale, Paris)

The London World's Fair—1862 (Sormani Palace, Milan)

Florence Nightingale's Life	Historical and Cultural Events
1907 December 7— Florence Nightingale is the first woman ever to be awarded Britain's Order of Merit.	
1910 August 13—Florence Nightingale dies at the age of ninety.	**1910** William Howard Taft becomes the twenty-seventh President of the United States. May—Jubilee celebrations are held at Carnegie Hall in New York to honor the fiftieth anniversary of the founding of the Nightingale School. At this time there are over 1,000 nursing schools in the United States.

A velocipede of 1869

Thomas Alva Edison and the phonograph he invented in 1876

BOOKS FOR FURTHER READING

Florence Nightingale by David Collins, Mott Media, 1984.

Florence Nightingale by Ruth Fox Hume, Random House, 1960.

Florence Nightingale by Charlotte Koch, Dandelion Press, 1979.

Florence Nightingale by Dorothy Turner, Watts, 1986.

Florence Nightingale by Lee Wyndham, The World Publishing Company, 1969.

Florence Nightingale: The Determined English Woman Who Founded Modern Nursing and Reformed Military Medicine by Charlotte Gray, Gareth Stevens, 1989.

Florence Nightingale's Nuns by Emmeline Garnett, Farrar, 1961.

FOR ADVANCED READERS:

Florence Nightingale by Elspeth J. Huxley, Putnam, 1975.

Florence Nightingale by Robin McKown, G.P. Putnam's Sons, 1966.

INDEX

(Continued on page 104)

INDEX *(Continued from page 103)*